Faxes to God

Faxes to God

REAL-LIFE PRAYERS
TRANSMITTED TO
THE HEAVENS

Joyce Shira Starr

HarperSanFrancisco
A Division of HarperCollinsPublishers

TO RAE AND REUBEN STARR
AND THE
SHEKHINA

Book design and illustration by Laurie Anderson.

———————————————————————

Library of Congress Cataloging in Publication Data
Starr, Joyce Shira.
Faxes to God : real-life prayers transmitted to the heavens /
Joyce Shira Starr.
p. cm.
ISBN 0–06–067585–3 (pbk.)
1. Intercessory prayer—Judaism. 2. Western Wall (Jerusalem)
3. Spiritual life—Judaism. I. Title.
BM724.S72 1995
296.7′2—dc20   94-40465

———————————————————————

95 96 97 98 99 ❖ HAD 10 9 8 7 6 5 4 3 2 1

This edition is printed on acid-free paper that meets the American National Standards Institute Z39.48 Standard.

Acknowledgments

I WISH to thank Isaac Kaul, director general of Bezeq, the Israeli telephone company, for his vision in creating a fax line to the Western Wall and for giving this book its initial wings by establishing a second fax line service.

Special gratitude to my agent, Karen Gantz Zahler, for embracing the creative and unconventional, and for her constant readiness to convey new ideas. To Harper Collins senior vice president Clayton Carlson, thank you for your confidence; and to editor Lisa Bach, my appreciation for your steady enthusiasm, encouragement, and wise counsel in bringing this book to life. I also want to thank Steve Hanselman, marketing manager at Harper San Francisco, for his thoughtful suggestions.

I am indebted to writer Frank W. Martin for his sage counsel on the craft of words and phrases. I also wish to thank Chaim Lauer, executive director of the Board of Jewish Education of Greater Washington, for sharing messages prepared by students and campers for their Western Wall project.

And to all who took the time to write and deliver messages—a humble thank-you indeed.

I wish to close with a personal note of gratitude to my family for faithfully understanding my dreams and goals.

Introduction

WELCOME to an alcove of heavenly hope, and to an offering of poignant, ardent, and warmly humorous messages from the alone to the Alone, via electronic ether.

This project took root when I learned that the Israeli telephone company, Bezeq, had established a fax service to the Western Wall of Jerusalem, the holiest site in Judaism. As the New York Times reported, "God has a fax number in Jerusalem."

Faxes to God was given birth when Bezeq agreed to install a second fax line for those willing to have their messages considered for this book, linking the writer's home, in effect, with the Western Wall of Jerusalem. The broadly announced new number, based on a sequence of 5s, offered distinct cultural protection against the "Evil Eye," or misfortune. People of all faiths, who might never have the privilege of visiting Israel, could now share in the power of the ancient stones of the Second Temple, destroyed in 70 C.E. Prayers from Jews, Christians, Muslims, and people of other diverse religious backgrounds began arriving daily. Missives were then carefully placed within the crevices of this sacred site.

Enter Celestial Cyberspace: Notices were then posted on Internet bulletin boards for spiritual "surfers" wishing to convey messages to the Man Above via this writer's e-mail address (and thereafter faxed to Jerusalem).

E-mail received ranged from the pious to the metaphysical. A student of theology wrote: "When two or three are gathered in His name, He's there. . . . Does an e-mail list count?"

Prayers and messages to the Almighty assume many faces: from sorrow to cheer, worry to whimsy, and anger to gratitude. If we are indeed made in God's image, then God too must have a sense of humor and irony. Prayers on high have included the desire for a date, a mate who enjoys chili peppers, and even pleas for a winning football team. In one striking instance, both mother and daughter reveal, through separate messages, a long-held, secret regret.

Children seem to raise more questions with God, succinct and pointed, but no less profound than the lengthiest prayer. Taken together, contributors to this book span almost a century of ages, from 3 to 93. May their prayers, messages, and questions be transmitted beyond the immutable Wall, past the gate of the new millennium, and on to that Divine setting where hope reigns supreme.

This book is a testament to the eternal significance—and, as one person so aptly described it, the "collective consciousness"—of the Western Wall of Jerusalem. It reminds us, above all, that even in an age of stellar communication, this ancient, sacred site yet gives root to our relationship with the Divine.

————

Approaching the Wall with his mother, a six-year-old boy watches as a dozen slips of paper suddenly fly from their resting places between the stones and flutter to the ground before them.

"When the messages fall from the Wall in this way," the child explains to his bemused mother, "it means that God has answered them."

A Short History
of the Western Wall

THE LORD told King David: "Your son, whom I will set on your throne in your place shall build the house for My name."

And thus, 480 years after the Israelites left the land of Egypt, in the fourth year of King Solomon's reign over Israel, approximately 962 B.C.E., Solomon "began to build the House of the Lord" atop Mount Moriah in Jerusalem.

And when, after seven years, the Temple was completed, Solomon convoked the elders of Israel "to bring the Ark of the Covenant of the Lord from the city of David, that is, Zion." The Lord then appeared to Solomon and said, "I consecrate this House which you have built and I set my name there forever."

Almost 400 years later, in 586 B.C.E., the King of Babylon, Nebuchadnezzar, attacked the Kingdom of

Judah, destroying the city of Jerusalem and the Temple of King Solomon. Most of the inhabitants were taken into captivity. Cyrus the Great, King of Persia, defeated the Babylonians in the middle of the sixth century B.C.E., and permitted the Jews to return to their homeland "to rebuild the house of the Lord."

Yet, according to the Prophet Jeremiah, those Jews who had remained in the Holy Land continued to worship at the ruins of the First Temple. The Temple was rebuilt on the original site in approximately 520–515 B.C.E., only to be sacked by the Macedonian king Antiochus IV in 170 B.C.E., in his campaign to crush Judaism.

The violation of the Second Temple provoked a successful Jewish revolt, beginning in the year 167 B.C.E., lead by General Judah Maccabaeus. The revolt underscored Jewish belief in the sanctity of this site.

Roman legions seized Jerusalem in 63 B.C.E., and the Roman senate confirmed Herod as King of Judea in 37 B.C.E. Herod took upon himself the challenge of rebuilding the Second Temple and did so in trumpeted splendor.

Chafing under foreign domination, a Jewish nationalist movement known as the Zealots challenged Roman control in 66 C.E. After a protracted siege launched by Vespasian, the Roman commander in Judah, but completed by his son Titus, Jerusalem and the Second Temple were destroyed by Roman legions.

The Western Wall alone survived their fiery wrath. Thus, this last fragment of "God's House" became sacred above all for the Jewish people.

Under the Emperor Hadrian (117–138 C.E.), Jews were forbidden to come within the sight of Jerusalem. They were permitted to mourn at the Wall once a year on Tish'a B'Av, the anniversary of the First and Second Temples' destruction, but only for a fee. Banishment from Jerusalem continued during Byzantine rule over Palestine.

Now a place of pilgrimage for bewailing the Second Temple's destruction, the Western Wall became known as the "Wailing Wall of Jerusalem." Jewish lore recounts that the Wall itself sheds tears on Tish'a B'Av.

The caliph Omar declared Jerusalem capital of the Arab realm of Palestine when his forces overtook the city in about 637 C.E., and he proceeded to construct Muslim holy buildings on the deserted platform of Mount Moriah.

Jewish pilgrims nevertheless continued to offer their prayers at the Temple ruins, as they would after the Christian Crusaders captured Jerusalem in 1099 C.E.

By the time Turkish sultan Salim conquered the city in 1517, the Wall was buried under more than a thousand years of rubble, and its exact location was unknown. Sultan Salim, according to Zeu Vilnay's *Legends of Jerusalem*, one day chanced upon an old Christian woman casting manure on a spot near his palace. Furious, he demanded that she be brought before him. The trembling woman explained that she had acted in obedience to the bishops, who ordained that a "mass of ordure" be brought once in thirty days and cast on the spot where the house of the God of Israel had formerly stood, for they wished it to be swamped and forgotten.

The sultan, learning that she spoke the truth, took coins of gold and silver and threw them into the dunghill. With shovel in hand, he urged the poor to follow his example and dig for the bounty. After ten thousand men worked for thirty days, the Western Wall — *Kotel ha-Maaravi* in Hebrew — was once again revealed. During British rule in the 1930s and 1940s, Muslims were declared the sole owners of the Wall, based on the belief that Mohammed's steed, Buraq, was tethered there during Mohammed's visit to the Temple Mount in a nocturnal dream.

Jews were granted access for devotional purposes, but no longer allowed to blow the shofar, a ram's horn used for sacred ceremonies—a searing humiliation. And during Jordan's twenty-year rule over the Old City and the Wall, from the 1949 armistice until the 1967 Six Day War, access to the Wall was forbidden to Jewish worshipers.

It was only when Israeli forces captured the Old City and the Western Wall on June 7, 1967, that the shofar again sounded God's praises at the site, the sole remnant of His Temple.

———

It is said that an angel of God revealed to Solomon that the Temple he was to build would be a temple of the people, belonging to all Israel. As recorded in the *Legends of Jerusalem*, Solomon was instructed to gather Israel together, and "let each one participate in the work according to his ability."

While the ministers, barons, priests, and Levites finished their work quickly, relying on the golden jewelry of their women, the cedar wood of Lebanon, and hired labor, the poor took much longer, for they could ill afford the materials, let alone hire workers to assist. Unlike the rich, they built the Western Wall with their own hands and tears.

And when the Temple stood completed, God brought his Divine Presence, the Shekhina, to dwell there. He chose the Western section, saying, "The labor of the paupers is dear to Me and My blessing will fall upon it."

A voice from heaven was then heard to exclaim, "The Divine Presence will never leave the Western Wall!" Thus, the Wall survived even when the Temple was destroyed.

FAXES TO GOD

Faxes to God

Dear God,

When are you coming down?

Serena,
AGE 3

Dear God:

Is it going to be OK for me to
laugh and giggle
when something goes wrong in heaven?
It has been my salvation on earth for
seventy-six years.

Can I keep my comfortable jeans,
or do you want me in white tie and tails?

Do I have to pray, once I get in?

Is there a place in heaven where
I can throw away all of my faults?

J. B.

1

Dear God,

Just give me an hour with the source code
to the Universe and a good debugger.

Ross

Dear God,

Can I be God?

Nathan,
<small>AGE 5</small>

Dear God,

When I am dead, can I be God?

Joey,
<small>AGE 5¾</small>

To: God
From: Giants Fans Everywhere

We thank you for saving the Giants from Florida, and sending us Peter Magowan and Walter Shorenstein.

We understand that you're still making amends to Atlanta for that whole Sherman's march thing, but have a heart.

The Giants really need to start winning.

Please let the Giants win the remaining games and put the Braves in a horrible slump. Amen.

Dear God,

Many years ago during a visit to Israel
I placed a note in the Wailing Wall
asking that my daughter not marry
before she gained the judgment
to find the right man.

Decades have gone by,
and my daughter is still single.
So what I would like to ask is whether
I could please take back my original request?
I pray to see my daughter
married this year.

        Estelle

Dear God,

My mother recently admitted placing a message
in the Wailing Wall almost twenty years ago
asking your help in ensuring that
I not marry until I achieved
the wisdom to find
the right man.

I wish
she had never made this wish.
But if it is not too late, please find me
the right man, and give me the good judgment
to spend the rest of my life with him.

                                        Rita

To the Wailing Wall:

God, it is a New Year and
I could use a little help here.

Abe

Dear Lord,

I am writing a special prayer to you today. This prayer is one for hope. I pray to you that all of the children of this earth will come to know you. Your light is a bright beacon shining for all.

Please let it shine extra bright for the little ones.

I love you.

June

Dear God,

I am so glad you are always looking out for me.

Max,
AGE 6

Dear God:

For so long I have been praying to you, over and over, for the same things. I see that you are slowly, gradually beginning to answer my prayers. Please do continue, and could things move a little less slowly?

Sandra

Dear God:

I'm really confused.
Why isn't life getting better?
Why does everyone I knòw seem to be depressed
and tired all the time?
Why couldn't you have made things
a little bit easier on all of us down here?

Why disease? Why hate?
Why rape and murder and lying and
mosquitoes and rotten fruit
and floods and famine
and
DO YOU REALLY LOVE US?

Why is my concept of love
so different from yours?
Why did you create us?
And if you can't answer these questions,

if I can never know the answers,
then why
did you make me capable of asking them?

Vivien

Dear God,

I have been wanting
to ask you this question:

Why isn't the world perfect?

Laura,
AGE 7

Dear God:

They say that money is the root of all evil. It sure would be nice to be just slightly evil.

Jack

To: God
Jerusalem, Israel

I ask that you have mercy
on those that wish to oppress others
and that you protect those peacekeepers
involved in the maintenance
of the peace in this world.
Grant these people the ability
to deal with those who wish to oppress
and the gentleness to show compassion
for those who are hapless victims.

Barnard

Dear God,

I wish you didn't let my rabbi die.

Jacob,
AGE 11

Dear God,

On this Christmas Day, my prayer, as always,
is of course for world peace and love.
I pray that we shape up
before you take it away from us
with very good cause.

On a strictly personal level,
I would pray to find a good man
to share my life,
an intellectual, a sensitive man
who loves the outdoors and hiking,
loves dogs, and loves cooking
as much as I do,
and would share my intense passion
for growing and eating chili peppers.

Ingrid

Dear God,

Why do girls not like boys and boys not like girls?

I wish they liked each other.

Julia,
AGE 8

Lord:

I just wanted you to know how much I love you and how grateful I am that you intervened to save my life eleven years ago.

Gordon

Dear God,

Thanks for saving my life
(you know what I'm talking about)
and please help me once more
(you know what I mean).

Love,

Terry

Dear God,

Thank you for letting my goldfish live a
long life.

> Justin,
> AGE 6

God,

With my wife gone many years now,
I ask that I be allowed to take a wife soon.
It is my fervent desire to share the joys
and happiness of life.

Donald

Dear God,

I understand that we are given shoulders
to bear what we must,
but there is a hole in my heart
carved by too many years of loneliness.

I ask in this New Year
to find a partner who will fill my heart
with your greatest gift: love.

Jolene

Dear Lord,

Please help our son to be a mensch and our
daughter to be happy.

Narley and Armida

Dear God:

Thank you, God,
for the most beautiful, strong,
and enduring love
that you have blessed Gregory and me with.
I pray that it will last forever,
and that our lives and our children's lives
will be blessed with good health,
happiness, and prosperity.
Thank you for enabling me
to earn such a good living,

to never know hunger
and to be able to give back
so much to others who do know hunger.

Teresa

Dear God,

Thank you for making me.

Carolyn,
AGE 3

Dear God,

I am happy that I am here.

Kara,
AGE 5½

Dear God,

Please bless my sister Mimi and cure her of
herpes. Also, please see if you can heal her knee.
I love her very much.

Freda

Wailing Wall:

Thank you, God,
for inventing my parents.

Adam,
AGE 5

Dear God,

Thank you for my wonderful family and for
keeping everyone healthy.

Sarah,
AGE 12

Dear God,

I hope for health and happiness for my family
and all of my friends for the rest of their lives.

Lesley

Dear God,

My parents are my best friends.

Every year that they remain on this earth
is a blessing.

Please share them with me as long
as you can.

Rhea

Dear God,

Please help my mother find friends in heaven.
She was so awfully lonely on earth.

Gert

Dear God,

When will there be world peace?

Rebecca,
AGE 11

Dear God,

We do not wish for the moon or stars.
All we want is peace.

Abe

Dear God,

Please try to make world peace so there will be no more wars and please find cures for AIDS and other sicknesses so people won't die.

Morgan,
AGE 11

Dear God,

Thank you for having my sister and thank you for letting me have my hamster.

Louis,
AGE 6

Re: The Wailing Wall

In the beginning,
there was nothing.
And god said:
"Let There Be Light."

And there was still nothing,
but you could see it.

       Mary Ellen

Oh God!

How do I keep in touch
with my spouse, Mary Jane,
after I arrive?

She's been so wonderful,
and we both hoped
to knock on your door together.

Is there some way I can signal
just to let her know
I am waiting?

Will Mother and Dad still love me
as much as I've missed and loved them
since they've been gone?

They gave me so much,
and taught me so much.
I still owe them everything.

                                    Jiggs

Dear God,

My grandpa has been gone since I was three.
How is he doing?

> Rebecca,
> AGE 8

Dear God,
Please don't call me.
I'll call you.

> Willy

Please, God,

see to it that a miracle will happen real soon
with the research of Alzheimer's, for the help
of my husband, Aaron.

> Mary

Dear God,

Give me the strength to take care of my wife.

Johnny

Dear God,

My prayer is for peace of mind and well-being for everyone I know and for everyone who knows everyone I know.

Molly

Dear Creator,

Let me lean on You for I can't do this alone.
I have felt alone for so long, so sad, so miserable.

I know that there are many that deserve your
kindness more than I, Lord, but as your child I
beg forgiveness and peace in your eyes.

I ask you to heal Bryan. He didn't ask for this
disease and he has not had the advantages to
be happy.

Lord, this disease has taken so much from him.
I know you must have your reasons and ours is
not to question why.

I know you are there, Lord.
Please heal my child as you have healed so
many before, a child that is truly without a father

27

and deserves a promising chance at life, to enjoy the wonderfulness of seeing your creations.

Once a sweet and loving child with many
dreams that could take a young man far,
he suffers so.

He is now shunned by so many.
Bring him back to us, Lord, healthy and whole.
Show him, Lord, that You are there so he knows
he is not alone.

Father, let your blessings reign in a family so overtaken by the ill things of this earth that there is no peace.

     Robin

Dear God,

Why do people die seemingly before their time?

Jack

To the Wall:

My Dearest most beautiful boy, Daniel,
Mimi and I love you so very much
and we think of you every day.

Since the day when you left,
nothing has ever been the same.
Know that you're the most loved boy ever.

Life was knowing Daniel,
living with Daniel, being with Daniel.

We love you forever.

    Mimi and Mami

My dear child:

You are in Heaven now
and do not have to see
the evils that man is doing
to the children.

The children are suffering so badly,
every day new children
are leaving—
Polly from Petaluma,
the little girl from Missouri,
and all the others
that were hurt and suffered.

Why is life so hard for America's children?
Why does God allow them to suffer?

Deborah

Dear God,

Thank you, God, for making a nice sun
and a nice rainbow
and a nice Mom.

Yoni,
AGE 6

Dear God,

Thank you for the air.

Shawn,
AGE 7½

Dear Lord,

My husband and I have been going through some terrible things lately, of which you know, and it almost seems as if there is a dark cloud hanging over us. I am asking you to remove the darkness that surrounds us and to help us see your light.

We are being notified today whether or not we will be approved for a home loan. I ask that you will help us to be approved, so that we can move into the home shortly. It is a humble home, Lord, and is in a nice neighborhood.

My husband can afford the payments and we need to move from where we are. I trust you, Lord.

I love you.

Jane

Dear G-d,

People think you made bad people. But I think
people just want to be bad.

> Mandy,
> AGE 7

Dear God,

I wish there were no violence. I wish nobody
killed anybody else.

> Samantha,
> AGE 7

Dear God,

I pray for our (me and the kids) rapid transition to Australia,
to finally be with my new husband and his children.

Thank you for helping my former husband to accept all this,
but I can't help but think that his acceptance
is just more proof of his lack of a backbone.

I always feared that if a criminal broke into the house,
he would hide rather than protect us,
or perhaps just sleep through it.
There is so much crime here,
and people are afraid—
even in this "nice" neighborhood.

I refuse to buy a gun, which means that I must always feel afraid and helpless or run from this madness for the sake of the kids.

I pray that in Australia we will be free of this constant, oppressive fear.

For Christmas and in general
of course I *must* conclude
by praying for peace:
in the Middle East, in Africa, in Bosnia,
but especially here on our own streets
and in our schools, where our children
are so threatened.

Nora

God,

Please try to put love in people's hearts.

If you don't the killing will continue.

I think that you need to have
a love for peace.

Eran,
AGE 7

Dear God,

Can you make no one homeless or sick?

Hannah,
AGE 7

Dear God,

I think there should be more peace than
violence in the world.

> Brian,
> AGE 9

Blessed Almighty Hashem,

Please grant peace for Israel,
the United States,
and all the other countries of the world.

Please help me get my old job back
working as I did before.

Please help me learn to be happy
and to be good to my family.

> Baruch

Dear God,

If I could ask You just one thing, it wouldn't be for world peace or for a perfect world because I know that those things are difficult to accomplish.

But I do ask to stop hunger. It is amazing to me how people in this world can watch the hunger go on and watch people die without feeling compassion. I would really like to see some of the wealthy people in this world who don't help with this issue experience what the poor and hungry people go through each and every day in their lives.

Heather,
AGE 11

Dear God,

You are more than one gender, aren't you?

Spencer

Dear God,

I pray that by at least the next millennium, women will be accorded as much space at the Western Wall as men.

Ruth

Dear God,

I raised our own four boys and one girl . . . and they came so fast that I always had two in diapers. One year I had a first grader, a kindergartner and four preschoolers. You remember, that was the year I babysat the Indian baby while her mother taught school in Wyoming.

Then they started growing up and could tie their own shoes and make their own bologna sandwiches and you found a brain-damaged teenager who needed special high school help for three years. I did that.

Now for years and years I have had this little granddaughter in the house and she is finally entering high school.

Just tell me one thing, God. Are you going to make me raise children until I get it right? Or is

it that I do get it right and that is the reason I am
chosen for this task?

Your tired servant,

Willo

Dear God,

I wish I had more time with my mom.

Susie,
AGE 10

Dear God,

Please let me dance at my daughter's wedding
and let my daughter have a child
who would know her grandmother at least
until she is two years old
and then, dear God,
I will be ready
to join you.

> Gita

Dear God,

May I be able to afford my wedding reception.

> Scott

Dear God,

Peace for Israel
would make my remaining days worthwhile.

May Israel make peace
with all of her enemies.

And could you please
show Israel
where the hidden oil is located?

David,
AGE 93

Dear God,

For a merciful God,
haven't you been hard on the Jews?

Manny

43

Dear God,

Where were you during World War II?

Lori,
AGE 11

Dear God,

If we are the chosen people, why are we mostly chosen for hatred and anti-Semitism?

Norman

Dear God,

Why did you let Hitler
kill all those Jews
in the Holocaust?

Sincerely,

Jeffrey,
AGE 10½

God,

I ask why the Holocaust happened, and why did
You not do anything about it?

Heidi,
AGE 12

God,

If you helped Moses out of slavery, why didn't
you help Jews in World War II?

> Aaron,
> AGE 12

Dear God,

I have been wondering if you are real or not.
Please tell me.
Love,

> Jonathan,
> AGE 9½

Dear God,

Isn't it time we figured out a way to eliminate war? Please help us.

Ron

Dear God,

I think we need peace.

Gary,
AGE 12

Dear God,

The media allots 90 percent of its news to stories of murder and strife. Couldn't you send us some good news?

Donna

Dear God,

Don't you get tired of hearing all our complaints?

George

In Regard to God . . .

My prayer is that everyone throughout the world will learn to find God within themselves through prayer, for we all have a direct line to Him. . . .

A lot of us do not even know that. . . .

I also pray that all the bad in this world does not get attributed to Him because He gave us autonomy over our lives by our OWN wills, our OWN decisions.

Thelma

Dear God,

I'm not selfish, but please let me grow. I'm too small. If you do, I'll be nice to my brother.

Love,

Suzanne,
AGE 6

God:

Boy, am I glad you're on-line.

I've been wanting to get in touch with you. I joined a group called "The Church of 80-Percent Sincerity," headed by your devotee, Reverend Dave. He said one rule of his church is that Mr. Kramer is in charge of parking, so I want to let you know Mr. Kramer is doing a swell job. Thanks to my calling on him for help, I get a parking place every day (and where I live, it is considered a small miracle).

49

I know, I know, I've been a bit critical of late
when I think of you. Truly, your Godship, have
you lost interest in the fabulous variety of your
creations here? It seems you started us up and
then hoped we would evolve on our own.

What you have here now is a gigantic *Lord of the
Flies* situation, your holiness. Earth is in a big
mess. For your convenience, there are lists avail-
able upon request concerning the species
presently in danger of extinction.

Of course, what's causing the danger is one of
your favorite species (or I thought we were at
one time), proving that Adam and Eve were pik-
ers when it came to wrecking their setup.

We probably are on the endangered list already.
I hope you're not too late looking into this. (You
can see us through the holes in the ozone layer.)

I thought you should know things are not at all
well for most people on this planet—that in

some areas of the globe, it is not worth being born a human: a cow or sheep has a better life.

This doesn't seem to be what you intended, your Grace. I probably shouldn't try to tell you your job, but I really think a few well-aimed lightning bolts might help.

> Stella

God,

Could you please help make people stop polluting?

> Dan,
> AGE 6

Dear God,

Why is New York City so trashy?

Jessica,
AGE 7

Dear God,

This prayer is for my brother-in-law. He is under-going heart surgery tomorrow. He is very dear to me and I pray for his surgery to be successful and for his speedy recovery.

Love,

Freda

Dear God,

I would like to know if there are any other forms
of life anywhere else in the universe or another
universe. And also if there ever will be a way for
all diseases to be cured.

> Joseph

Dear Lord:

Please let me totally conquer this disease with
your help.

> Robert

Dear God,

I have been wondering this for a while:
What is death?

> Seth,
> AGE 10

Dear God,

Please give my daughter the strength to pull herself together and make a new life for herself (soon).

And please give Dale the strength to deal with her, and to continue having enough strength in reserve to love me, and to take care of his children.

And give me the patience and health and peace of mind to know that everything will work out for the very best with Dale and I. And I really hope I can calm my anxiety over all this. Please give me the strength as well.

Love,

Dannie

P.S. And please continue to let my father watch over me from heaven or wherever.

Dear God,

Thank you for the love of our two gifted children.

May I live to see them happy and successful. And please help my daughter find her true love.

Sam

Dear God,

I really don't believe in faxing to God, but what do I have to lose? I call upon you as last resort; please help me find the woman of my parents' dreams (and mine).

Joaqim

Dear God,

Please bless the marriage on which we are about to embark. The lifelong journey that your word outlines is the path we shall walk.

Please, God, guide us.

Jeff and Silvey

Good morning, God.

Everything seems to be going well and I don't want to seem superstitious, but thanks for your "guidance," God.

I especially need your help now, though, in overcoming several major problems this month.

Please help me.

Bill

Dear God,

Look down on the enemies of compassion
and smile at them
with your sword of love.

> Peter

Dear God,

Why are you invisible?

> Alexandra,
> AGE 6½

Subject: the . . . upstairs

The man/woman? upstairs would be swamped
even at a terminal of 100,000 baud,
let alone the 2,400 baud
which most of us use today.

There are 5,000,000,000 plus people on the
earth today.
There are 86,400 seconds in one day.

At 100,000 baud
that allows for 10,000 characters per second
or 864,000,000 bytes per day,
which gives each person
less than one byte per day.
This obviously won't do.

Those who have been to the other worlds
have seen how prayers
rise from earth to God.

Prem

Dear God,

Do you ever get lonely?

Jeff,
AGE 10

Dear God,

They say that love conquers all.
After almost sixty years with my wife,
I am a true believer.

Thank you for this blessing.

Ruben

Dear God,

You have done so much for me. Thank you.

Alana,
AGE 7

59

Lord,

Love me, forgive my mistakes.

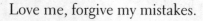

Maria

Lord:

Give me the strength to become the person
I wish I could be.

Brian

The Wall:

Please grant me peace, prosperity, wealth,
temperance, happiness, love,
patience, compassion, and balance
in all things.

Give me the guidance
to become the best person
that I am capable of being.

Thank you.

    Theresa

Dear God,

Words can never say
how much the love of my daughter
has meant to me. I thank you.

    Ben

Dear God,

In spite of my ups and downs,
I could not begin
to count my blessings.

Thank you,

Michael

Dear God,

Why is it that idealists are so often pursued by
contradiction and paradox into hypocrisy?

Heath

Dear God,

May we never need financial help from anyone.

Morris

God:

Just once help me win the Florida Lotto.

Henry

Dear God,

I sit here at this computer in the security of my home.

Having read about the military atrocities motivated by generations of revenge, I wonder, are they more sinful than me?

Phil

Dear God,

Thank you for making me what I am today.

David,
AGE 8

Dear God,

Cheer up.

There are worse things than being slammed by a German philosopher.

S. R.

Dear God,

I know I've paid little or no heed in recent years.

I have no right to ask anything for myself, and in fact would not bother you on my own account.

Likewise, I would not make this request on behalf of my step-daughter, who is a thinking, reasoning adult and should be able to live with the consequences of her own actions or inactions.

I will, however, make this request for my grandson, who is two years old.

Tyler James is on this earth through no fault of his own, by no request of his, and is an innocent, loving, and precious person.

He truly belongs to you, Lord.

The request is to help his mother recognize the responsibility she has to provide for Tyler. Make Amy see that benefits are earned through effort, and welfare is provided by working.

As parents, we can assist and guide her, but she is beyond the point of being provided for.

If there is a way for you to awaken the desire to succeed and the will to persist, please help Tyler by giving Amy this gift.

Joseph

To God's Ear:

My truest and deepest belief is that God must have the greatest sense of humor of all time.

My life is a testament to God's sense of the ridiculous and tricksterism.

There is balance in all things and a creativity in chaos; thus, my message to God is a thank-you as well as a criticism.

Shasti

Dear God,

Thank you for making me in my family.

Keith,
AGE 7

Dear God:

As you brought redemption to Sarah
late in life
by giving her a son,
I offer you boundless thanks
for the miracle of life
bestowed upon us
after eight years, fifteen in vitros, and extensive
surgery.

It was all worth the wait.

I have a fetching one-year-old son
and a beautiful, soulful, newborn daughter.

                                        Karen

Hi God,

This is Sygal again.
My exams are coming up.

I pray that You will give me
the patience to sit and study
(actually, the study part is no problem,
but I can't sit still
for more than five minutes and concentrate,
so the "sit" part will be appreciated).

I'm in the neuroscience program at Hebrew
University.

Dear God,

I thank You for all blessings and would like your
assistance in finding a committed relationship,
ideally with Chip.

Regina

Dear God,

Please help me see love at first sight.

Cecille

Dear God,

Why is the grass green?

How did you make the clouds?

What do you eat?

Danny,
AGE 4

Dear God,

I hereby ask for your help in eliminating lethal disease, including AIDS and cancer. Thank you.

Andy

Dear God,

Please help make the world a better place to live in for my generation and future ones.

Sharon,
AGE 11

Dear God,

I pray that your mercy extends to cats.
My beloved Jeshuran needs yet another
operation.

A playful, happy, and pure spirit,
he is a joy in my life.

Protect Jeshuran against more troubles
and anesthesia
than his little body should have to bear.

And please
do not let him die.

       Jo

Dear God,

The overseas work assignment you helped me obtain means that I must either leave my beloved cat at home (which is out of the question) or take him with me. I understand that travel by plane can be very dangerous for an animal. Would you please protect my Jessie from radiation, air pressure, and insensitive airport personnel? Thank you in advance.

Judy

Dear God,

My cat is eleven and cats only live to be fifteen. I wish he would live longer.

Lauren,
AGE 8

G-d,

Please let Abbey survive the cold luggage area on the plane. And God, let Wiski live, and let Brittany get healthy from her infected bug bite.

Galit,
AGE 9

Dear God,

I wish that my parents would get back together and Amber would still be alive, and we would still have Sasha, Sammy, and Max.

In other words: a perfect life.

Kira,
AGE 9

I wish to ask G-d for things He cannot give us.
Peace and understanding are what I pray for.

But we must work ourselves to acquire them.
We must help G-d help us.

Sara Joy

Dear God,

I want the game Commander King.

Ellie,
AGE 5

Dear God,

Why did You choose to create each person differently?

More specifically, what is the purpose of creating such complex personalities in each individual?

Was it perhaps to teach us how to love one another?

> Annie

Dear God,

I wish I could talk to you.

> Helen,
> AGE 8

Dear God,

I wish I could see you in person.

Love,

Marissa,
AGE 9

Dear God,

One day I wish I could hear you.

Steven,
AGE 10

To: God

I have been thinking about this subject for some time now, and I can boil the questions and answers down to a minimalist Q & A. The question will be one asked by countless wise or foolish people through the ages, and the answer the same.

Question: Why?

Answer: Because.

Frank

Dear God,

I would like to know where the dead people are.

Shawn,
AGE 8

Dear God,

I hope that my son, Robert, and my husband, Arnold, are at peace and together.

Respectfully,

Judy

Dear God,

Thank you for giving me such a wonderful brother, who was like a father to me. He was the kindest, sweetest person I ever knew.

Having neither father nor mother, he made my life livable, and tried to fill the emptiness with joy. Please thank him for all the good he did for me. I have missed him terribly since he departed over twenty years ago.

Rachel

Dear God,

Thank you for the gift of a brother who pro-
tected, led, challenged, and helped me to aspire.

He fed me when I was young; force-fed me
when I grew, with learning and music. Sometimes a haven, sometimes a wall, but always
there for me. This is family.

Wendy

Dear God,

Where are you living right now? Can you die?

Andrew,
AGE 8

Dear God,

Thank you for guiding me and imbuing me with the spirit and passion for volunteer work.

Thank you for the friends who by example taught me and inspired me to follow the paths that I have.

Thank you for the gift of singing, which has brought me so much pleasure and I hope others joy.

    Helen

Dear God,

Thank you for school, so we can learn.

              Hallie,
              AGE 8

Dear God,

There are so many people in need of a blessing.
Please give them health and happiness for the
good that they do in this life.

Ethel

God:

I wish no evil against my neighbors, in spite of
their misdeeds.

Donald

Dear God:

It is my life's dream to work in Hollywood. Is there a chance you could convince Steven Spielberg to phone *my* home?

Asherah

Dear Wall,

I can't believe I'm actually sending a fax to God, but here goes.

I recently started channeling via autowriting, and it turns out that some beings (not all) actually can come through via autotyping.

I am *not* nuts or a kook or a religious freak. I have a degree in the hard sciences from an Ivy League university, and if anyone had told me I'd be doing this a year, even a month, ago, I would have sprained something laughing at them. I just barely believe this myself. But it's happening. (First rule of the experimental scientist: Never spit in the eye of a fact.)

So for whatever it's worth, here is what I channeled from a being who calls herself Clemennia. It's about the nature of the universe (which they refer to as 'allone'), which is held together by supreme love.

Punctuation and some capitalization have been added for clarity; they're not too good with that sort of thing.

Mar

"Allone, light—is same thing;
talk, not talk, love feel same
Allone be love, hold,
sharetalk,
not talk.
Say all love, no time, no body,
only feel love.
Verse of love, verse of water,
flow, flow pattern.
All see, feel, verse, allone."

Clemennia

Dear God,

I wish for chocolate-chip cookies.

Elaine,
AGE 2½

Dear God,

This is Florida calling. I know we prayed for
rain, God, but not for the Deluge. Either send
us another ark, or stop the waters.

Bart

Lord,

I ask that you help us to succeed in our business
and that you bless my loving husband tenfold.

I praise you, Lord, for the baby in my womb.

Susan

Lord,

I humbly and faithfully implore you to grant Frank freedom from smoking and bring the lover I desire into my life.

> Joanne

Dear God,

Please help make me wise and successful, as my need to provide for my family is my only life force.

Mike

Western Wall:

Please pray that I meet a nice guy (mensch). I
am thirty-one years old and have been looking,
waiting, and dating. No such luck. I want to fall
in love, get married, and have children. Thank
you for everything.

Ron

Wailing Wall:

On this Christmas Day,
my prayer, as always,
is for world peace and love.

There is no reason for us to hate one another,
to shoot one another, to discriminate on any
basis whatsoever. This is the only world we have,
and we need to make the best of it.

I pray that all the weapons of destruction
will in an instant evaporate
and beautiful fragrant flowers will take their
place,
to bring joy to those who behold them.

Danny

Dear Lord:

Thank you so much for watching over me and
my surgery and for its success. Everyone who
sees the incision states what a good job Dr.
Sandler did. But I know he was merely the
hands, or tool, for your inspiration.

Your son,

Robert

Dear God,

You are very special.

Naomi,
AGE 6

Dear God,

You are very good to us.

Emily,
AGE 7

Oh Lord, God of heaven and earth, we worship and praise your grace. Please show us your will in our lives and in a way that we can understand.

Please watch over and protect our children and help us teach them in your love. Your goodness and grace are beyond our comprehension; please grant us a glimpse of your greatness so that our faith may be strong.

Anne and Don

Dear Lord:

Thank you for your blessings on my family and friends.

Ellen and Gilda truly appreciate the good news with regard to their health. Please continue to keep them well and in your thoughts.

Please also look out for my nephew, Richard. He is such a good and loving child. Tomorrow he is going back to Johns Hopkins University because of pains in his heart. I wish I could go with him, but I have to get ready for my own surgery on Thursday.

Thank you for allowing me to get over the virus. Please keep me in your thoughts and blessings when the pathology report has to come back.

My wife and I pray to let the news be good so that we can continue to raise Scott, our ten-month-old son. I appreciate all you can do!

Your son,

Robert

Dear God,

Thank you for keeping my husband and myself
well and on our own two feet, especially when
we see so many of our friends who were once
so healthy now having to use wheelchairs
and canes.

      Perl

God watches over all the earth.

           Tamar,
           AGE 4¼

Heavenly Father,

who lives inside the hearts
of each of your sons and daughters,
help us to learn about your love
and the care you have for all of us.

Teach us to be humble, and guide us
to your greatness.

> Adda

Dear God,

May the Third Temple become a reality.

> Isaac

Wall built of tears and Mother earth,
filled with fears and hopes,
desires and passion.

Wall of Compassion, Wall of Love
made of collective consciousness,
if you could,
what would you say?

Cassandra

I love you, God.

Craig,
AGE 7